This is a Carlton Book

Published in 2016 by Carlton Books,
an imprint of the Carlton Publishing Group,
20 Mortimer Street, London W1T 3JW

Colour treatment by Rupert Van Wyk and Vida Williams

Additional photo on page 8 (top left) © photograph
by Christopher Simon Sykes, Camera Press London and
pages 8 (centre left) and 6-7 (centre) © photograph by
Eamonn McCabe, Camera Press London.
All other photographs courtesy of iStockphoto.com,
Shutterstock.com and courtesy of The Roald Dahl Museum
and Story Centre, Great Missenden.
Illustrations of bird pie and BFG suitcase by Danny
Baldwin. Illustrations of snozzcumbers, glue pot,
glass eye and magic potion by Mark Walker.

ISBN: 978-1-78312-215-8

Printed in China

Executive Editor: Bryony Jones
Design Director: Russell Porter
Design Manager: Emily Clarke
Designer: Ceri Hurst
Photoshop Designer: Punchbowldesign.com

RECIPE

WONKA VITE

of of a manticore
unk (and the suitcase)
of an elephant
lls of three eggs
a whiffle-bird
rom a wart hog
r of a cow
d horn)

The BFG
Royal Dream Blower

OFFICIAL RESIDENCE:
Giant's Green, Windsor Great Park
TEL: 976 1008   FAX: 976 1007

Roald Dahl was a spy, ace
fighter-pilot, chocolate historian
and medical inventor. He was also
the author of "Charlie and the
Chocolate Factory", "Matilda",
"The BFG" and many more brilliant
stories. He remains the World's
No.1 storyteller.

GIANT PEACH
★ADMITS
PLEASE do not to
BZ 086478

No 2S
FORMULA 86
Delayed Action
Mouse-Maker

Roald Dahl said, "If you have good thoughts they will shine
out of your face like sunbeams and you will always look lovely."

We believe in doing good things. That's why ten percent of all Roald Dahl income*
goes to our charity partners. We have supported causes including: specialist
children's nurses, grants for families in need, and educational outreach programmes.
Thank you for helping us to sustain this vital work. Find out more at roalddahl.com.

The Roald Dahl Charitable Trust is a registered UK charity (no. 1119330).
* All author payments and royalty income net of third party commissions.

The Gloriumptious Worlds of ROALD DAHL

Illustrated by
Quentin Blake

Written by
Stella Caldwell

CARLTON
BOOKS

Your guide to the Worlds of Roald Dahl

It all began here...

The Writing Hut

Clever Mr Fox, eccentric Willy Wonka and the wicked Grand High Witch first came to life in a hut in Roald Dahl's garden. This was no ordinary shed. Instead it was filled with photographs, pictures and weird and wonderful objects which sparked Roald's imagination.

FANTASTIC FAMILY -----------

Like Mr Fox, Roald was close to his family. His father died when he was just three, and his Norwegian mother raised Roald and his siblings. *"She told us stories about Norwegian trolls and all the other mythical creatures that lived in the dark pine forests, for she was a great teller of tales."*

SCHOOL ------------------

When he turned nine, Roald went to boarding school. He hated the bullying and harsh punishments - no prizes for guessing where he got all his ideas for Crunchem Hall and the ghastly Miss Trunchbull!

Roald always wrote in pencil on a yellow pad of paper.

FIGHTER PILOT ----------------

Flying through the sky – like James in his giant peach – was a delight for adventurous Roald. He joined the Royal Air Force in World War Two: *"It was truly the most breathless and in a way the most exhilarating time I have ever had in my life."*

FAMILY LIFE --------------------

Just as Danny lives in an old gipsy caravan, Roald had one in his back garden for his family to play inside. The author adored his five children and loved to tell them magical stories – tales that turned into his books.

Chapter One

Magic and Mayhem

Roald Dahl's books are full of
incredible magic and mischief.
He created unforgettable adventures
out of ordinary things: a juicy
peach could become a home for
gigantic insects; or a humdrum
factory could turn out to be the
start of a chocolatey adventure!

As a young man, Roald ate a bar of chocolate every day as part of his lunch. He would roll the foil wrapper from each bar into a silvery ball, small at first, but gradually getting bigger and bigger...

James and the Giant Peach

After James loses his loving parents to a hungry rhinoceros, he is forced to live with his beastly aunts Spiker and Sponge. When a mysterious old man hands James a bag of beautiful crystals, however, events take a peculiar – and magical – turn...

James Henry Trotter, Age 7

3d

RUNAWAY RHINO DEVOURS SHOPPERS

Staff reporter Bill Hyde

Two people were killed by a rhinoceros after it escaped from London Zoo yesterday afternoon.

The enraged animal galloped along busy streets, charging startled pedestrians and ramming vehicles.

Witnesses described how the rhino gored and consumed its victims – named by police as Mr and Mrs Trotter – in less than 35 seconds: "Fortunately, their ordeal was over in a jiffy," said shop-owner Mr McGraw.

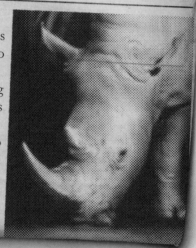

What if a cherry just *kept* on growing and growing?

Or an apple?

Or a lovely squishy peach?

Spiker and Sponge

Could any child have two more loathsome aunts than tall and bony Spiker or her enormously fat sister, Sponge? These repulsive sisters treat poor James like a slave, forcing him to do all the housework and never allowing him to see other children.

'Behold MY gorgeous curvy shape,
my teeth, my charming grin!
Oh beauteous me!
How I adore
My radiant looks!
And please ignore
The pimple on my chin.'

Aunt Spiker

'I look and smell,'
Aunt Sponge declared,
'as lovely as a rose!
Just feast your eyes
upon my face, observe
my shapely nose!'

Aunt Sponge

SPIKER AND SPONGE'S

HOUSE RULES

FOR THE DISGUSTING LITTEL BRAT

1. IT IS FORBIDDEN TO LEAVE THE GARDEN FOR ANY REASON.

2. COOKING, CLEANING, WOODCUTTING ETC, ARE TO BE CARRIED OUT BETWEEN THE HOURS OF 6AM AND 9PM EVERY DAY. LAZINISS WILL NOT BE TOLERATED.

3. CRYING AND OTHER INFANTILE BEHAVIOUR IS NOT PERMITTED.

4. DISOBEDIENCE WILL RESULT IN BEING LOCKED UP WITH THE CELLAR RATS!! OR A BEETING.

How about a really hideous witch who wants to cut off James's legs in exchange for these?

The Magic Crystals

When James encounters the strange old man in his aunts' garden, it seems his troubles are over. Given a bag of sparkling green crystals, he is told that "*fabulous, unbelievable* things" will happen if he swallows them. As he runs off, however, James trips beneath an old peach tree – and can only watch as the precious crystals wriggle away into the soil...

'Something is about to happen,' he told himself. 'Something peculiar is about to happen at any moment.'

JAMES HENRY TROTTER

Spell No. 41

CROCODILE CRYSTALS

❋ USE WITH CAUTION ❋
– will cause rapid enlargement in all living things!

Boil one thousand long slimy crocodile tongues in the skull of a dead witch for twenty days and nights with the eyeballs of a lizard.

Now add the following:
The fingers of a young monkey
The gizzard of a pig
The beak of a green parrot
The juice of a porcupine
Three spoonfuls of sugar

Stew for a week and leave the moon to do the rest.

'It's growing!' Aunt Spiker cried.
'It's getting bigger and bigger!'

The greedy aunts soon spot an opportunity to make some quick cash.

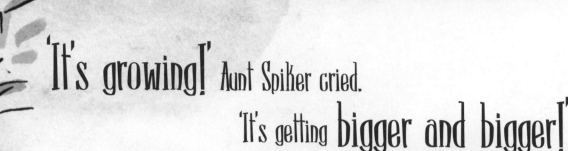

GIANT PEACH 1/-
★ADMITS ONE★
PLEASE do not touch or bite the peach!
BZ 086478

EXTRAORDINARY, ENORMOUS PEACH!

MUST BE SEEN TO BE BELEEVED!

ADMITTANCE:
JUST ONE SHILLING!*

HALF PRICE
FOR CHILDREN
UNDER SIX WEEKS OLD!!

✱ PAY dOUBLE
TO BRING CAMERA.

News of the giant peach brings swarms of reporters to the house.

Miraculous sight! – mammoth peach
just touching ground, nearly as tall
as tree, perhaps wide as house...

Skin very beautiful, butter yellow,
pink & white patches.
Perfectly ripe.

Swarms of people vying for a glimpse,
journalists everywhere
plus helicopters etc.

(Strange set-up, two old ladies in charge,
one very fat, the other skin & bones.
Spooky house on top of a hill, barred windows!
Sure I saw a child peeking out.)

The Adventure Begins

James discovers a hole in the side of the peach, and can't resist crawling through the squishy tunnel. Inside, several gigantic insects have been waiting for him – and soon he and his new companions are rolling away from the ghastly hill on a marvellous and magical journey.

REPORT FROM THE SHIP'S DOCTOR

I was called to the bridge at around 3 p.m. The First Officer informed me that a round ball had been witnessed hovering overhead and the men speculated it might be a weapon. At this point, the captain appeared to start hallucinating. On examining the ball through his telescope, he told the assembled officers that he could see "a little boy in short trousers" moving on top of it. He then became visibly distressed, screaming that he could also see monstrous insects including a "giant ladybird", "a colossal green grasshopper" and an "enormous centipede". At this point, the ball disappeared behind a cloud and was seen no more.

It is my medical opinion that the captain is suffering from nervous exhaustion, and he has been sedated and removed from duty until further notice.

L. Wallace

Signed: Dr Lionel Wallace,
4 September, 8:30 p.m.

Like the idea of a _flying_ peach.

And magical, sinister cloud men who control the weather & make hailstones etc?

The sight of the flying peach and its unusual passengers causes much alarm down below.

The peach was a soft stealthy traveller, making no noise at all as it floated along. And several times during that long silent night ride... James and his friends saw things that no one had ever seen before.

Across the Ocean

Drifting silently through the night, the peach – carried by a giant flock of seagulls – travels across the Atlantic. The passengers face many dangers, from treacherous waters to the sinister Cloud-Men. But the night is also full of wonder, for James and his companions see things that they will never forget.

The Centipede's boots are ruined after a Cloud-Man throws fast-drying rainbow paint all over him.

New Science Journal ... ISSUE 147

eathermen Intrigued "Cloud-Men"

R HIS MIRACULOUS APPEARANCE
d a flying peach, James Henry Trotter has
household name. And meteorologists the
have been fascinated by the youngster's
of "Cloud-Men".

ly these "cotton-wool" creatures were first
ing pieces of cloud and rolling them into
rbles".

described how the Cloud-Men – angered
entipede shouting "Half-wits!" and other
t them – began to pelt the unfortunate
crew with the hailstones.

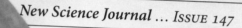

...er's sketch of a "Cloud-Man" has caused a stir amongst scientists.

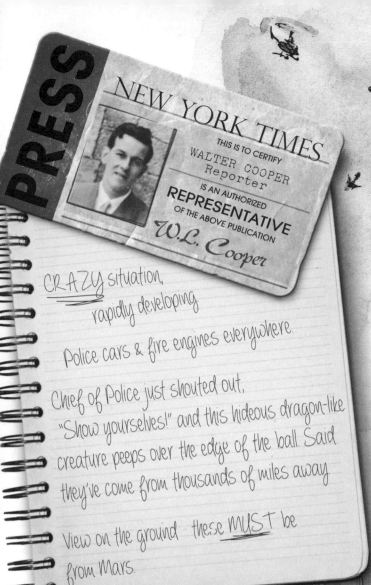

CRAZY situation,
rapidly developing

Police cars & fire engines everywhere.

Chief of Police just shouted out,
"Show yourselves!" and this hideous dragon-like
creature peeps over the edge of the ball. Said
they've come from thousands of miles away

View on the ground these MUST be
from Mars.

Land!

After their long night of adventure, James and his companions are delighted to spot land below when daylight finally breaks. Skyscrapers glisten in the morning sunshine, and James suddenly realizes that they have crossed the Atlantic Ocean – and reached America.

THIS IS AN EMERGENCY ACTION NOTIFICATION (EAN) DIRECTED BY THE PRESIDENT OF THE UNITED STATES. ALL STATIONS MUST URGENTLY BROADCAST THE FOLLOWING MESSAGE:

A BOMB IS CURRENTLY HOVERING OVER THE CITY OF NEW YORK, AND RESIDENTS MUST IMMEDIATELY TAKE COVER IN CELLARS OR SUBWAY STATIONS.

FORTHCOMING MARRIAGES

HEAD OF NEW YORK FIRE DEPT AND LADYBIRD

The engagement is announced between Reginald Sparks, son of Wanda and Ted Sparks, and a giant ladybird from England.

UR SUMMERS AND
RAE

Journey's End

Once James assures the gathered spectators that he and his companions mean no harm, they are greeted on the streets of New York like heroes. And for all of them, it is really just the beginning of a new journey – one that leads to success and happiness.

HANDMADE FOOTWEAR

FOOTSTEPS
High Class Boot & Shoe Manufacturers

Centipede
Vice-President-
in-Charge-of-Sales

The enormous peach stone becomes a famous monument in Central Park, as well as James's house.

The Magic Finger

Mr Gregg and his sons love to hunt wild ducks and deer. However, the girl who lives on the farm next to theirs just can't stand it! One day she spots the family out hunting, and before she knows it she's turned the Magic Finger on them – and unleashed all sorts of trouble and trickery.

Teacher in "Dark Magic" Claim

Primary-school teacher Mrs Winter is suing her employer for what she terms "witchery" after she suddenly grew a bushy tail and whiskers in class.

Mrs Winter claims the bizarre transformation happened "in a flash" during an English lesson, and says she is struggling to come to terms with her new appearance.

The girl had promised herself she would never use the Magic Finger again – not after what happened to her teacher, Mrs Winter!

'And suddenly a sort of **flash** comes out of me, a quick flash like **something electric.**'

The morning after their hunting spree, the Greggs awake to find they have grown duck wings.

After swearing to throw away their guns for good, the Greggs are given a second chance. But that's not the only thing they change.

DEED OF CHANGE OF NAME

I, Mr Gregg

HEREBY DECLARE

To relinquish the use of my former name Mr Gregg and have adopted for all purposes the name of Mr Egg.

Dated this 5th day of June, 1965

Mr Egg

By the above named Mr Egg

UK DEED POLL SERVICE

DEED OF CHANGE OF NAME

Esio Trot

Lonely Mr Hoppy has two great loves: his balcony flowers and widowed Mrs Silver who lives in the apartment below his. Unfortunately for him, Mrs Silver gives all her love to her tortoise, Alfie. That is, until Mr Hoppy comes up with a *marvellous* plan to make Alfie a bigger and better tortoise...

Mr Hoppy wouldn't have minded
becoming a tortoise himself
if it meant Mrs Silver stroking his shell each morning and whispering endearments to him.

Mr Hoppy tells Mrs Silver that this African spell (read the words backwards!) will make Alfie grow faster.

ESIO TROT, ESIO TROT,
TEG REGGIB REGGIB!
EMOC NO, ESIO TROT,
WORG PU, FFUP PU, TOOHS PU!

Alfie
(weight 13 ounces)

Tortoise no. 8
(weight 27 ounces)

For several weeks, Mr Hoppy secretly replaces Mrs Silver's pet with a slightly larger tortoise.

Mr Hoppy buys a total of 140 tortoises from 14 different shops.

When "Alfie" doubles in size, love blooms for Mr Hoppy and Mrs Silver.

GREAT SNAKES EXOTIC PETS
Find your perfect companion today!

40409

CUSTOMER ORDER NO.		DATE	
00065737		17.08.1989	
NAME			
Mr Hoppy			

	QUAN.	DESCRIPTION	PRICE	AMOUNT
1	10	dark-shelled tortoises:		
2	3	Small	10.00	£30 00
3	4	Medium	15.00	£60 00
4	3	Large	18.00	£54 00
5				
6				
7				£144 00

19

Danny the Champion of the World

Danny's wonderful father tells magical stories and exciting ideas fly off him like sparks However, Danny discovers a shocking secret: his dad loves to poach pheasants! This soon leads the pair into adventure as they dream up a rather marvellous poaching plot...

Danny's father should know the countryside like the back of his hand. How exciting for a child to find out that the death head moth squeaks!

'Poaching is such a fabulous and exciting sport that once you start doing it, it gets into your blood and you can't give it up!'
DANNY'S FATHER

Victor Hazell

Danny and his father live in an old gipsy caravan behind a filling station. Here, Danny first meets the rude and sneering Victor Hazell when he sweeps up in his huge Rolls Royce. Mr Hazell, a rich landowner, stocks his wood with fattened pheasants for the shooting season – and Danny's dad would *love* to teach him a lesson.

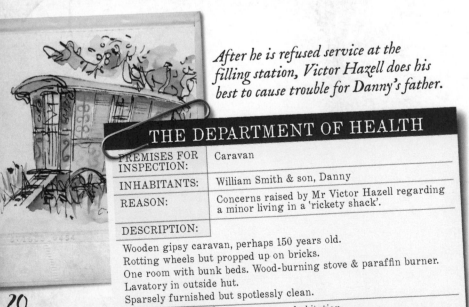

After he is refused service at the filling station, Victor Hazell does his best to cause trouble for Danny's father.

THE DEPARTMENT OF HEALTH

PREMISES FOR INSPECTION:	Caravan
INHABITANTS:	William Smith & son, Danny
REASON:	Concerns raised by Mr Victor Hazell regarding a minor living in a 'rickety shack'.
DESCRIPTION:	
Wooden gipsy caravan, perhaps 150 years old. Rotting wheels but propped up on bricks. One room with bunk beds. Wood-burning stove & paraffin burner. Lavatory in outside hut. Sparsely furnished but spotlessly clean.	
CONCLUSION:	Fit for human habitation.
INSPECTOR:	Gordon Winterbottom

World's Best Poaching Methods

FACT: Pheasants adore raisins.

Method 1: The Horse-hair Stopper
Soak a few raisins overnight. Slit them with a knife and push through horse-hair cut into half-inch lengths. Scatter on ground. Swallowed raisins will tickle pheasant's throat & bird will become rooted to the spot.

Method 2: The Sticky Hat
Twist paper into a small cone and smear inside with glue. Insert a few raisins and place cone in a small hole in ground. Pheasant will pop head into hole and come up wearing hat over eyes. Unable to see, it won't move an inch!

The Sleeping Beauty

Danny bravely rescues his injured dad from a pit in Victor Hazell's wood – a nasty trap set for poachers. Doc Spencer (who, it turns out, enjoys the odd bit of poaching himself) tends to the patient's broken ankle and prescribes sleeping pills. When Danny sees the capsules, he has a marvellous idea...

MR VICTOR HAZELL
REQUESTS THE PLEASURE OF THE COMPANY OF

Godfrey Grenville, Duke of Buckingham

AT THE GRAND OPENING-DAY SHOOT
AT HAZELL'S WOOD ESTATE

ON 1 OCTOBER AT 10 A.M.

RSVP: THE SHOOTING LODGE, HAZELL'S WOOD ESTATE, BUCKINGHAMSHIRE

Danny's "Sleeping Beauty" method involves pouring sleeping-pill powder into raisins, and then sewing them up. Pheasants love raisins!

℞ Prescription

FOR: William Smith
DATE: 16 September

Sleeping capsules, 10mg x 50
Take ONE capsule, just before bed.

The Great Escape

Danny and his father manage to bag 120 birds, and hide them in a specially built pram. When the drugged birds start to wake up, they perch on the filling-station roof. This surprises everyone – including Victor Hazell, who happens to be driving past in his Rolls.

Perambulator: Extra-large Poacher's Model
– SKETCH ONE –

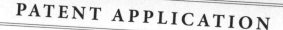

'Get those birds off my car!' Mr Hazell bellowed.
'Can't you see they're ruining the paintwork?'

PATENT APPLICATION

DATE: 10.02.1976
INVENTOR: Mr William Smith

DESCRIPTION

Perambulator: Extra-large Poacher's Model
Long, extra-wide perambulator with very deep well. Carries a baby as well as concealing up to 100 pheasants or other similarly sized animals. Sheet-covering hides birds as well as serving as a comfortable baby mattress.

21

Charlie and the Chocolate Factory

When Charlie Bucket wins a Golden Ticket to visit Willy Wonka's chocolate factory, he and four other winners enter a world of marvellous inventions and edible delights. But inside this sugary maze, the likes of greedy Augustus Gloop and spoilt Veruca Salt are in for some nasty surprises...

Charlie Bucket

Charlie's Family

Charlie, his parents and four grandparents all live together in a tiny, two-roomed house. Only Mr Bucket has a job, screwing on toothpaste caps in a factory, and the family never has enough to eat.

Possible ticket winners...
Augustus Pottle
& Miranda Grope
— fall into choc river
Violet Strabismus
— gum chewer

WONKA FACTORY TO BE OPENED
AT LAST TO LUCKY FEW!

Mr WILLY WONKA, the confectionery genius whom nobody has seen for the last ten years, sent out the following notice today: *I, Willy Wonka, have decided to allow five children – just five, mind you – to visit my factory this year.*

Marvellous Surprises

As news of Mr Wonka's hidden Golden Tickets spreads, the whole world becomes caught up in a chocolate-buying frenzy. The first child to strike gold is Augustus Gloop, a boy so plump he looks like he has been "blown up by a powerful pump". Following hot on his heels are rich Veruca Salt, gum-chewing Violet Beauregarde and television-crazy Mike Teavee. Poor little Charlie Bucket can only dream of such fantastic luck...

25 January 1964

Tattle
& Bystander 2s.6d   Weekly

At home with peanut factory heiress and golden-ticket winner Veruca Salt

15 January

Tomorrow's my birthday, and I'm hoping for another Wonka bar. There's been nothing but cabbage soup for weeks now and I keep imagining the taste of chocolate melting over my tongue. And oh, how tremendous it would be to find a golden ticket!!

Well, I didn't get a ticket in my birthday bar, but HE found one! → And Grandma Georgina says the last ticket will probably go to some nasty little beast who doesn't deserve it...

ONLY ONE GOLDEN TICKET LEFT!!

The Teavee household was crammed with visitors this afternoon, all hoping to catch a glimpse of lucky winner Mike Teavee.

However, the pistol-toting youth seemed extremely annoyed by all the fuss as he attempted to focus on a gangster shootout on television.

'IT'S THE FIFTH GOLDEN TICKET... AND I'VE FOUND IT!'

CHARLIE BUCKET

Grandpa Joe – who hasn't been out of bed for 20 years – does a victory dance when he discovers Charlie's good fortune.

Mr Willy Wonka

Extraordinary and eccentric, Willy Wonka is the most amazing chocolate maker the world has ever seen. A magician when it comes to inventing sweet concoctions, Mr Wonka delights in making mischief – but he's no fool when it comes to deciding what his young factory visitors deserve.

And oh, how clever he looked!
How quick and sharp and full of life!

'Mr Willy Wonka can make marshmallows that taste of violets... He can make chewing gum that never loses its taste, and sugar balloons that you can blow up to enormous sizes before you pop them with a pin and gobble them up.'
GRANDPA JOE

HENRY HEATH

105-107-109 OXFORD STREET. W

TOP HATS
IN THE MOST BRILLIANT SILK PLUSH

PRICES: FROM **42** /-

WHY WEAR AN ILL-FITTING HAT?
VISIT HENRY HEATH FOR A
HEAD MEASUREMENT TODAY!

BY APPOINTMENT TO
HM THE QUEEN

AGENTS THROUGHOUT THE WORLD ※ WRITE FOR ILLUSTRATIONS OF NEW SHAPES

TROUT HALL ACADEMY

Rt Hon Humphrey Cruddock MP
The Home Office

16 April

Dear Mr Cruddock

I am writing with regard to the latest Willy Wonka invention, Spotty Powder. As you will no doubt be aware, this substance causes users to erupt in bright red spots.

This week alone, almost a quarter of my pupils have been absent from school with "Chicken Pox". I suspect Spotty Powder is the more likely cause.

This rubbish can't be sold to children, it's criminal! If the government does not take action soon, I believe Willy Wonka could bring down the entire school system.

Yours sincerely,

Henry Piker

Mr Henry Piker
HEADMASTER

CHILDREN! Look out for WILLY WONKA'S INVISIBLE Chocolate Bars

Just perfect for eating in class!

WONKA'S TREATS

WILLY WONKA'S Spotty Powder

For Spots Like the Pox!

24

Marvellous Surprises

When the big day finally arrives, Mr Wonka is almost as excited as his guests. As the great factory gates clang shut behind the visitors, they are whisked away into a deep maze of passages. Inside, the muffled roars of distant machinery echo through the corridors and fantastic smells of burnt sugar, melted chocolate, mint and violets waft through the air.

PRESS PASS

WONKA'S FACTORY,
1 February

Freezing day – huge crowd pushing & shoving.

Violet – still chomping!

Augustus – simply ENORMOUS
(Must eat non-stop)

Veruca – spoilt little brat
in silver mink

Mike Teavee – regular Lone Ranger
covered in toy pistols
(looks pretty crazy)

Charlie – skinny little shrimp
(poor kid shivering)
& grandfather like a skeleton!

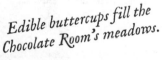

Edible buttercups fill the Chocolate Room's meadows.

The Chocolate Room

The first stop is the all-important Chocolate Room. The door opens upon a beautiful valley, cut through by a great chocolate river and lined by sugary meadows. Here, the astonished visitors catch a glimpse of Wonka's workers, the singing and dancing Oompa-Loompas – and it is here that Augustus becomes the first visitor to find himself in a spot of trouble...

'Augustus Gloop! Augustus Gloop!
The great big greedy nincompoop!'
THE OOMPA-LOOMPAS

After Augustus tumbles into the river, he finds himself sucked up a pipe – and on the way to the Fudge Room.

The Inventing Room

Like a witch's kitchen, the inventing room is filled with sizzling pots and pans, and strange splutters and gurgles. It is here that Mr Wonka works on top-secret inventions including the most "*amazing* and *fabulous* and *sensational* gum in the whole world" – though as Violet discovers, it is not yet quite ready for use.

'I don't want a blueberry for a daughter!' yelled Mrs Beauregarde. 'Put her back to what she was this instant!'

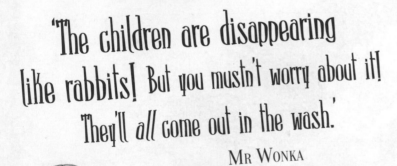

"The children are disappearing like rabbits! But you mustn't worry about it! They'll all come out in the wash.'

MR WONKA

After Veruca is judged to be a "bad nut", she is shoved down a rubbish chute.

Mr Wonka,

I am writing to complain about the vile treatment meted out to Veruca, my wife Angina and me in your so-called Nut Room.

Veruca wanted a squirrel and I was quite prepared to pay for it — and look what happened! The poor, defenceless girl was attacked by a hundred squirrels and shoved down the chute like rubbish. And then the beastly vermin had the nerve to go for my wife and me too!

Have you any idea what it was like sliding down that chute fully expecting to be sizzled like a sausage at the end of it? Or to end up covered in rancid slime? Disgusting!

I have informed my lawyers. You'll pay for this, Wonka!

Mr Salt

The buttons on the lift, from top to bottom, read:
THE ROCK CANDY MINE – 1,000 FEET DEEP
CAVITY-FILLING CARAMELS, NO MORE DENTISTS
TELEVISION CHOCOLATE
EXPLODING SWEETS FOR YOUR ENEMIES
STICKJAW FOR TALKATIVE PARENTS
UP AND OUT

The Great Glass Lift

Mr Wonka's sugar-powered lift is no ordinary elevator, and can go sideways, longways and slantways. There are rows and rows of buttons, each one directing the lift to a marvellous destination. When Mr Wonka tells Charlie and Mike Teavee they may each pick one button, it isn't long before Mike Teavee has found the label reading "Television Chocolate"!

Mike Teavee's determination to be "sent by television" has some unfortunate consequences for the boy.

Up and Out!

As the last child standing, Charlie discovers that he has "won" – and that there's no time to lose! Before he knows it, he and Grandpa Joe are back in the lift and Mr Wonka has pressed the UP AND OUT button. As the elevator shoots up through the factory roof and into the sky, it is the start of a marvellous new adventure...

'Well *done* Charlie...! Now the fun is really going to start!'

MR WONKA

The Great Glass Elevator

Charlie is now the proud owner of the chocolate factory. When he, his family and Mr Wonka hurtle up into the sky in the Great Glass Elevator, they accidentally enter Earth's orbit. Here, they encounter not only the newly built Space Hotel USA but also the most murderous creatures in the entire universe.

SPACE HOTEL USA IN ORBIT!

AFTER ITS THRILLING LAUNCH from Cape Kennedy yesterday morning, Space Hotel USA is now orbiting Earth at a height of 240 miles.

The luxurious hotel has been called the "marvel of the space age" by President Gilligrass, and rumours are flying that he will be one of its first guests.

Meanwhile, the Transport Capsule, manned by Bud Shuckworth, Lenny Shanks and Chad Showler, is also orbiting Earth and is expected to link up with the hotel shortly.

Space Hotel USA – Safety First

SPACE TOURS LIMITED

SPACE HOTEL USA

space, the final frontier, is the perfect destination for adventurous travellers! Stay at the sumptuous Space Hotel USA, and become one of the lucky few to experience the mystery and magnificence of space – in guaranteed safety, comfort and style.

★ TOUR HIGHLIGHTS ★

★ Look down on Earth, in all its cosmic splendour, from the comfort of your room!

★ Stylish accommodation includes a heated swimming pool and tennis courts

★ No need to float with our state-of-the-art gravity-making machine!

★ View Vermicious Knids and other aliens in total safety from the viewing platform.

AVOID DISAPPOINTMENT AND BOOK TODAY!

★ SPACE HOTEL USA, New York 10016

WOULD YOU KNOW A VERMICIOUS KNID IF YOU SAW ONE?

Native to the planet Vermes, the deadly **Vermicious Knid** may appear in many guises. In its natural state, the Knid resembles an enormous egg with two blazing eyes. However, this beast is a cunning shapeshifter and may take *any* form it wishes – from a human to a horse.

Be KNID-AWARE and look out for:

★ Slimy and wrinkled green-brown skin
★ Saucer-like eyes with red pupils
★ A murderous expression

If in doubt... **SCRAM!**

The Battle of the Knids

Back to the Chocolate Factory

Following the great Battle of the Knids, the Glass Elevator streaks back to Earth. After towing the Transport Capsule to safety, the elevator crashes through the roof of Charlie's chocolate factory. Here, three of the grandparents remain confined to their bed, though Mr Wonka has a cunning plan to get them moving again.

> 'I haven't been out of this bed in twenty years and I'm not getting out now for anybody!'
>
> GRANDMA JOSEPHINE

RECIPE
WONKA-VITE

The hoof of a manticore

The trunk (and the suitcase) of an elephant

The yolks of three eggs from a whiffle-bird

A wart from a wart-hog

The horn of a cow (it must be a loud horn)

WONKA-VITE
EACH PILL will make you YOUNGER by exactly 20 years.

⚠ CAUTION!
Do not take more than the amount recommended by MR WONKA.

The Time Travels of Grandma Josephine

Taking more Wonka-Vite pills than advised has some troubling results for Grandma Josephine. When she becomes minus-two in age, Charlie and Mr Wonka must pay a visit to the eerie world of Minusland to rescue her. Here, Josephine's ghostly shadow is sprayed with Vita-Wonk – making her the oldest person in the world. Thankfully, Mr Wonka sorts out the mess.

Age 78

On the way to age minus-two

Age 352

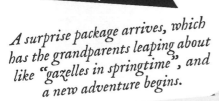

A surprise package arrives, which has the grandparents leaping about like "gazelles in springtime", and a new adventure begins.

THE WHITE HOUSE
Washington

To Mr Willy Wonka

SIR
Today the entire nation, indeed the whole world, is rejoicing at the safe return of our transport capsule from space with 136 souls on board. Had it not been ~~help they received from an unknown spaceship,~~ come back. It has

Wonka
~~Cho~~olate Factory
~~ro~~ad
~~ENGLA~~ND

Chapter Two

Beastly Adults

From George's witchy grandmother to the terrifying Trunchbull, Roald's stories are full of cruel and nasty adults. But as Roald also said, "Beastly people must be punished!"

A rather gruesome object in Roald's writing hut was his very own hip bone! When he had an operation to replace his hip, his doctor said it was the largest he had ever seen.

The Twits

It is hard to imagine two more spiteful characters than Mr and Mrs Twit. This vile couple delight in playing beastly tricks on each other, and in mistreating any child or animal that happens to cross their path.

In pub. Beer stealing. An old boy dropped his glass eye into the tankard. He then saw it looking up at him.

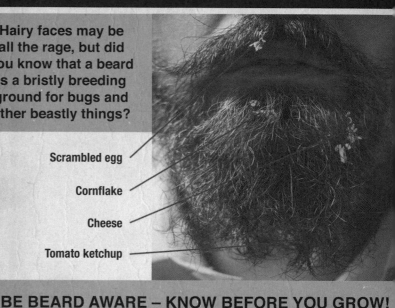
2 DESCRIPTION

PASSPORT OFFICE
15 FEB 1985 RH
274
LONDON

Profession	Monkey trainer
Place of birth	England
Date of birth	13 June 1942
Height	5 ft 7 in
Colour of eyes	Murky brown
Colour of hair	Black/grey
Peculiarities:	Profuse beard; hairy nostrils and ear holes; twit
Usual signature of bearer:	Mr Twit

2 DESCRIPTION

PASSPORT OFFICE
15 FEB 1985 JW
274
LONDON

Profession	Monkey trainer
Place of birth	England
Date of birth	3 May 1945
Height	4 ft 8 in
Colour of eyes	Steely grey (one eyed)
Colour of hair	Black/grey
Peculiarities:	Glass eye; squint; wonky nose; protruding teeth
Usual signature of bearer:	Mrs Twit

'I told you I was watching you,' cackled Mrs Twit.

'I've got eyes everywhere so you'd better be careful.'

Home Sweet Home

Mr and Mrs Twit live in a windowless house set in a garden of spiky thistles and stinging nettles. Far from being welcoming hosts, The Twits' main concern is to keep "nasty nosey children" *out*.

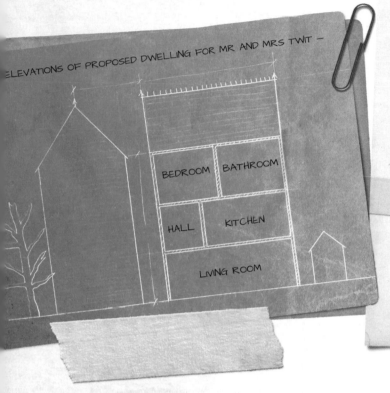

ELEVATIONS OF PROPOSED DWELLING FOR MR AND MRS TWIT —

BEDROOM   BATHROOM

HALL   KITCHEN

LIVING ROOM

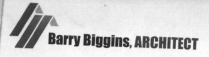

Barry Biggins, ARCHITECT

Dear Mr Twit

Further to our recent meeting, it gives me great pleasure to include my initial plans for your new home.

May I once again suggest that you include at least one or two windows? I fear that without them, you and Mrs Twit may find the house rather dark.

I look forward to hearing from you.

Yours sincerely,

B. Biggins

B. Biggins

Mr Wiggins

Please proceed with the "no windows" plan. Who wants every Tom, Dick and Harry peeping in to see what you're doing?

Ever,

Mr Twit

Some house! It looks like a prison.

I'll wipe that silly laugh off your beaks!

I'll get you next time, you filthy, feathery frumps! I'll wring your necks, the whole lot of you, and have you **bubbling in the pot for Bird Pie before this day is out!**

MR TWIT

Tasty Bird Pie

12 plump birds (prefer blackbirds, jenny wrens, robins – but any sort will do)

A handful of slugs (Mr Twit loves 'em!)
1 chopped onion
2 chopped carrots
2 pints brown sauce
Suet pastry dough (roll into 2 sheets)

METHOD

* Pluck the birds
  (leave heads, wings & legs on for extra crunch)
* Place birds & slugs in suet-lined pudding bowl
* Cover with vegetables & pour over brown sauce
* Cover with pastry lid & tie bowl up in a pudding cloth
* Steam for 3 hours

Bird Pie

Every Wednesday, the Twits enjoy a very tasty meal. By painting a tree with Hugtight glue – the world's stickiest – Mr Twit ensures there are always enough trapped birds for his wife's flavoursome pie.

HUGTIGHT

THE STRONGEST GLUE KNOWN TO MANKIND

CAUTION!
STICKS ANYTHING... AND EVERYTHING!

The Twits keep a family of monkeys caged up in their garden. It is Mr Twit's dream to own the first upside-down monkey circus.

Muggle-Wump and the Roly-Poly Bird

Muggle-Wump, the head of the monkey family, is pretty fed up of his upside-down lifestyle with the Twits. However, things start to look up when the magnificent Roly-Poly Bird makes a surprise visit from Africa.

When the Roly-Poly Bird prevents Mr and Mrs Twit from having their usual bird pie, things turn rather nasty. The Twits are bent on revenge, but they haven't counted on Muggle-Wump's clever idea: to show them just how sticky Hugtight glue can be!

RARE AFRICAN BIRD SPOTTED IN SUBURBS

Ornithologists yesterday flocked to the site where a rare African Roly-Poly Bird was spotted flying above English homes.

More likely to be seen in the jungles of deepest Africa, the magnificently plumed Roly-Poly Bird normally roosts in orange trees and is attracted to berries – of all description.

Specialists were at a loss to explain the bird's extraordinary appearance in the northern hemisphere. Dr R. Grouse of the Birdwatchers' Society joked: 'Perhaps this Roly-Poly Bird fancied a holiday and some British strawberries.'

'Now we'll never get free! We're stuck here forever!'
MRS TWIT

POLICE REPORT
DEPARTMENT OF MISSING PERSONS

MISSING PERSON/S: Mr and Mrs Twit

DATE OF DISAPPEARANCE: Unknown; reported 4 January

NARRATIVE

Mr Fred Black of the gas board called round at the home of Mr and Mrs Twit on January 4 to read the meter. After receiving no response, Mr Black pulled open the door and saw two piles of clothes on the floor, along with two pairs of shoes and a walking stick. He called the police who attended the property the same afternoon.

PECULIAR CIRCUMSTANCES:

Living room furniture stuck to ceiling.

The investigation is ongoing.

George's Marvellous Medicine

Eight-year-old George's "grizzly old grunion" of a grandma is about as beastly a person as you could imagine. She gripes from morning to night, and never has a kind word to say to anyone. George dreams of exploding Grandma away, and when he is left alone with her one morning, he invents a very special medicine for her...

Grandma

With her stained teeth and puckered-up, dog's-bottom mouth, Grandma is not the sort to enjoy a game of Snakes and Ladders with her grandson or take any interest in him whatsoever. However, she does enjoy taunting George with her nasty snippets of "wisdom"...

GRANDMA'S WISDOM

Like laziness and greed, growing's a nasty, childish habit. Never grow up, always down!

Eat cabbage THREE times a day – and preferably with caterpillars in it.

Fat earwigs are extra tasty – but you have to crunch them before they bite you...

'Some of us have fire on our tongues and sparks in our bellies and wizardry in the tips of our fingers.'
GRANDMA

Grandma has been ordering me about again, moaning about everything and giving me her beastly advice. I really think she might be a witch! Oh, how I wish I could do something – perhaps put a firecracker under her chair or slip a slithery green snake down the back of her dress? Something WHOPPING.

'Give me another dose, my boy, and let's go through the roof!'

GRANDMA

A Surprise for the Krankys

George's medicine is certainly a marvellous concoction. When Mr and Mrs Kranky return home, it is to find a gigantic hen strutting around the yard and Grandma's head sticking through the roof of the house. Mr Kranky, who has been trying to breed bigger and bigger animals for years, is quick to spot a business opportunity...

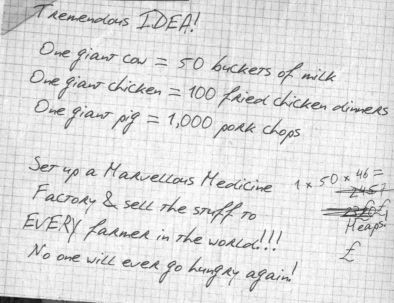

Tremendous IDEA!

One giant cow = 50 buckets of milk
One giant chicken = 100 fried chicken dinners
One giant pig = 1,000 pork chops

Set up a Marvellous Medicine Factory & sell the stuff to EVERY farmer in the world!!!

No one will ever go hungry again!

$1 \times 50 \times 46 =$ ~~£457~~
~~£240£~~
Heaps!
£

THE CRANE COMPANY
Peter Winchworth

Servicing ALL Your Lifting Needs Since 1952

THE CRANE COMPANY
×1952×

INVOICE

INVOICE # 0017392

DATE: 3 May 1980
BILL TO: Mr Killy Kranky, Kranky Farm

DESCRIPTION:

Extra-large crane, plus two operators (out-of-hours service)
Successful removal of one larger-than-average human from the roof of Kranky Farm

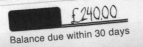

£240.00

Balance due within 30 days

Mystery at Kranky Farm

PARANORMAL INVESTIGATORS have been called in after several members of the public reported seeing a "giant woman astride a giant horse" in the vicinity of Kranky Farm.

The witnesses – who were all walking or driving in the area early on Saturday afternoon – called the police after seeing the massive horse leaping over trees and scaling local buildings.

Shocked witness Gerry Mole described how the mystery rider shrieked, "Stand back all you miserable midgets!" as her giant mount galloped along a country road. He described her as "shrivelled, hag-like and unbelievably tall".

Medicines Two, Three & Four

The only problem with Mr Kranky's "big idea" is that the magic medicine needs to be made again – and George needs to remember *exactly* what went into it. This leads to a few hiccups along the way...

Magic Medicine Number ②

'Oh my sainted aunts,'
cried Mr Killy Kranky.

'We've got it wrong! This chicken's no good to anybody! It's all legs! No one wants chicken legs!'

Magic Medicine Number ③

'Who wants a chicken with a long neck? You can't eat a chicken's neck!'

Magic Medicine Number ④

Grandma was less than happy with her transformation from

glorious giant to miserable midget.

MISSING

HAVE YOU SEEN THIS WOMAN?

NAME:
Grandma

AGE: 89

LAST SEEN:
Kranky Farm, 5 May

This much-loved family member vanished from her home without trace on 5 May. Grandma needs medication four times a day, and her family is very worried about her.

Anyone with information should contact the police on 671 47

39

Matilda

Matilda Wormwood is a genius. She could speak perfectly before she was two, and had read Charles Dickens's *Great Expectations* by the age of four. However, most of the adults around her either ignore her or think all children are "nauseating little warts". Luckily for Matilda, she discovers she has a very special magical power...

She went to Africa with **Ernest Hemingway** and to India with **Rudyard Kipling.**

She travelled all over the world while sitting in her little room in an English village.

823/.8
PR4567.A2 H67

AUTHOR Dickens, Charles

TITLE Oliver Twist

Date Due	Borrower's Name
DEC 9	Betty Grimwig
FEB 01	Martha Moore
MAR 24	Walter Crook
APR 21	Matilda Wormwood

— GREAT MISSENDEN

Mr and Mrs Wormwood

Buck-teethed Mr Wormwood is a second-hand car salesman whose motto is, "No one ever got rich being honest." Infuriated by Matilda's love of reading, he calls her an "ignorant little squirt". Meanwhile, bingo-loving Mrs Wormwood thinks girls should concentrate only on their appearance. As she tells Miss Honey, "You chose books. I chose looks."

Do I make Matilda a wicked child with lovely parents, or a lovely child with wicked parents?

CUSTOMERS ARE THERE TO BE DIDDLED

After her father's mysterious death, the orphaned Miss Honey was cared for by her aunt, Agatha Trunchbull.

Tricking The Trunchbull

When Matilda visits Miss Honey's home and discovers the strange story that lies behind her teacher's poverty, an idea for getting rid of The Trunchbull once and for all begins to form in her mind.

COMMUNITY STUNNED BY DOCTOR'S SUDDEN DEATH

GREAT MISSENDEN – Villagers have been left shocked by the "unexplained" death of Dr Magnus Honey at his home yesterday afternoon. The much-loved doctor had served the community for over 20 years.

I, Miss Jennifer Honey, agree to pay my legal guardian, Miss Agatha Trunchbull, the full amount of my teaching salary for a period of ten (10) years starting from the date below.

In return, I will be provided with a weekly allowance of one pound (£1).

Signed: Jennifer Honey _____ *J. Honey*_

Signed: Agatha Trunchbull _____ *A. Trunchbull*

Date: 3 September 1986

TELEKINESIS: the supposed ability to move objects through mind power alone is termed telekinesis or psychokinesis. Although there are many who claim to have witnessed the phenomenon, scientific evidence remains elusive.

ABOVE. During the late nineteenth century, Victorians clamoured to witness Edmund Troutbach demonstrate his telekinetic powers.

I've looked up my power in an encyclopedia and it's got a name – TELEKINESIS! I've been practising it like mad, and I managed to lift a cigar at least 6 inches up into the air earlier.

I've had an idea – if I can get a bit of chalk to write all on its own on the blackboard then I can make The Trunchbull think it's Magnus's ghost!

Agatha, give my Jenny back her house.

G+A GUNN & ABEL SOLICITORS

Dear Miss Honey

It gives me great pleasure to inform you that this morning, the Last Will and Testament of your late father, Dr Magnus Honey, mysteriously appeared in the post.

This document reveals that you have been the rightful owner of your father's property, The Red House, since his death. It also states that the substantial sum of his lifetime savings was left solely to you.

When her parents flee the country, Matilda finds a happy home with Miss Honey.

Chapter Three

Fantastic Beasts and Beings

Roald Dahl loved writing about animals, from wicked wolves to fantastically smart foxes. His stories also feature many strange beings, such as terrifying witches, man-eating giants and the delightfully jumbly BFG.

Roald enjoyed writing about all sorts of creatures, from huge giants to tiny tortoises. That might explain why he kept a tiny wooden tortoise in a jam jar on his desk.

The BFG

When the Big Friendly Giant (the BFG) plucks Sophie from her orphanage bed, it's as well for her she hasn't fallen into the hands of the Bloodbottler – or any of the other human-eating giants. Sophie and her new friend soon hatch a plan to capture the bloodthirsty giants – but it will require the help of the Queen of England!

Been thinking that the BFG of "Danny the Champion" surely deserves a book of his own?!

VILLAGE ORPHANAGE

DORMITORY RULES

* Beds must be made immediately upon rising (at 6am)

* Clothes are to be kept <u>perfectly</u> folded and crease-free

* Leaving your bed for <u>any</u> reason after lights-out is STRICTLY FORBIDDEN

* REMEMBER: Children should neither be seen nor heard!!

THOSE WHO BREAK THE RULES WILL BE LOCKED UP IN THE CELLAR WITHOUT FOOD OR WATER!

The Witching Hour – A special moment in the middle of the night when every child and every grown-up is in a deep sleep, and all the dark things come out from hiding and have the world to themselves.

The Dreamcatcher

The giant who "kidsnatches" Sophie during the witching hour is no ordinary giant. While other giants guzzle humans, the "nice and jumbly" BFG survives on snozzcumbers and frobscottle. The BFG has made it his mission to capture dreams – and nightmares – in Dream Country so that he can pass on sweet dreams to sleeping children.

The BFG's amazing ears can pick up all the secret whisperings of the world as well as the "buzzy-hum" of passing dreams.

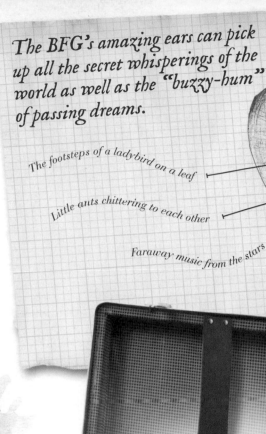

The footsteps of a ladybird on a leaf

Little ants chittering to each other

Faraway music from the stars

'Dreams is very mystical things,' the BFG said. 'Human beans is not understanding them at all.'

The BFG uses a trumpet to blow sweet dreams into the bedrooms of sleeping children.

Freddie's Diary
KEEP OUT!!!

NAME: Freddie Jones

AGE: 8

BEST FRIEND: Toby Higgins

BEST THINGS: Football, conkers, choclate

WORST THINGS: Anna (yukky sister),
bad dreams.

5 January   Last night I dremt I made myself an awesome pair of suction boots, and when I put them on I could walk strate up the kitchun wall and upside down across the ceeling! So, Anna came in and started shouting at me like she usually does – What do you think you're doing up there?!!!!

So I told her, "I said you were driving me up the wall & now you've done it!"

Ha, ha, ha – if only it were true, that would teach her.

'You is seeing them in the distance **but just wait till you get them close up.**

Those giants is all at **least fifty feet tall** with huge muscles and cockles alive alive-o.

I is the titchy one. I is the runt.'

THE BFG

It was not in the least difficult to believe that this ghastly brute ate men, women and children every night.

Giant Country

After Sophie is snatched from her bed, the BFG makes off with the child wrapped in a blanket. Galloping through the night at tremendous speed, the giant seemingly crosses oceans and strides over rivers and mountains until at last Sophie glimpses a strange and desolate wasteland. This barren place – dotted with blue rocks and dead "skeleton" trees – is Giant Country, home to the BFG as well as nine colossal man-eating giants.

The Giant's Guide to HUMAN BEANS

⇒ TASTE ⇐

Not all human beans taste like strawberries and cream.

Why not journey to the following places to sample the many and diverse flavours of the world's humans?

World Map

Labrador – hint of the Great Dane!

Sweden – sweet and sour.

Denmark – taste of dogs (labradors to be precise).

Wales – a little fishy.

Greece – avoid! Horribly greasy.

Turkey – juicy and flavoursome.

Jersey – woolly tasting (a bit like a cardigan).

Panama – strong taste of hats!

Chile – refreshingly cold.

Wellington, New Zealand – especially delicious (taste of boots).

WELLINGTON DA

SEVEN FARMERS – AND THEIR WELLIES – MISSING!

Staff reporter Russell Clarke

Police are mystified by the disappearance of seven farmers yesterday evening.

The farmers were all working late in their barns or fields when they vanished. To add to the mystery, their clothes were found at the various scenes although in all cases their Wellington boots had also disappeared.

THE GIANTS OF GIANT COUNTRY

*By Professor Cornelius Stickleback,
Institute for Giant Research*

DRINKING HABITS

EXTENSIVE OBSERVATION IN THE FIELD HAS REVEALED that the inhabitants of Giant Country drink nothing but "Frobscottle", a pale green substance of uncertain origin. The bubbles of this gaseous liquid travel *downwards*, a phenomenon that researchers are still at pains to understand. Frobscottle may be described as having a vanilla-and-cream taste with hints of raspberry. Although delicious, the thunderous "whizzpoppers" – as the giants name them – that follow soon after drinking may prove socially awkward for humans.

JOURNAL OF LITTLE KNOWN BEASTS 115

'It's disgusterous!'
the BFG gurgled...

'Try it yourself,
this **foulsome
snozzcumber!**

Gobblefunk

The BFG squiffs and squiddles his words around though somehow Sophie always know *exactly* what he means. The BFG never had the chance to go to school, but by borrowing a copy of *Nicholas Nickleby* (by "Dahl's Chickens") from a boy's bedroom, he has educated himself in the ways of the English language.

The BFG shows Sophie his book "borrowed" 80 years previously!

49

'I can't stand it! Just think of those poor girls and boys who are going to be eaten alive in a few hours' time! We can't just sit here and do nothing! We've got to go after those brutes!' SOPHIE

The Queen's Nightmare

Sophie's scheme for outwitting the bloodthirsty giants has the BFG mixing together a frightful nightmare – about girls and boys being snatched from their school beds by giants – to blow into the Queen of England's bedroom. When this terrible trogglehumper is ready, the BFG and Sophie travel by night to Buckingham Palace.

When the queen hears the dreadful morning news, she realizes that her nightmare may have been more than just a dream...

The Time

EIGHTEEN GIRLS VANISH MYSTERIOUSLY
FROM THEIR BEDS AT ROEDEAN SCHOOL!

Fourteen boys disappear from Eton!
Bones are found underneath dormitory windows!

Parents nationwide are keeping their children at home following the shocking disappearance of pupils from two of the country's top boarding schools.

The grisly finds of human remains beneath the pupils' dormitory windows has only fuelled the horror.

One dormitory survivor described seeing a "massive hand, many times the size of a human's" reaching in through the window, though his comments have been attributed to extreme shock.

'Oh Majester!'

cried the BFG.

'Oh, Queen! Oh, Monacher!

Oh, Golden Sovreign!...

Oh, Sultana!...'

BUCKINGHAM PALACE

URGENT – *For the attention of Mr Tibbs*

8.00 am. – The Queen requests that her visitor, a 24-foot giant, be seated for breakfast with her Majesty in the Great Ballroom within the next half hour.

(One normal-sized child will also be present).

After some quick thinking, Mr Tibbs the butler succeeds in seating his unusual guest for breakfast.

Rather like the idea of the BFG wearing sandals like my own!

AIRFORCE IN SECRET MISSION

ONLOOKERS STOOD AGOG TODAY AS NINE HELICOPTERS THUNDERED ACROSS THE BRITISH ISLES IN PURSUIT OF WHAT APPEARED TO BE A GALLOPING GIANT.

Several witnesses reported glimpsing "a small child wearing glasses" in the giant's right ear, while two more described how the giant wore "sandals".

THE ROYAL AIRFORCE

SECRET

MISSION TO "GIANT COUNTRY"

Concerning the RAF's recent mission to airlift 9 giants from this "terra incognita", I can confirm that Giant Country occupies no known space in any atlas. I observed that we had already left the very last page of the atlas before arriving at our destination over an hour later. Clearly a team of explorers should be sent as soon as possible.

FLIGHT LIEUTENANT TOMMY HOPKINS
NAVIGATOR

IT IS FORBIDDEN TO FEED THE GIANTS

Dear Visitor
These giants are kept on a strict diet of snozzcumbers, and those attempting to feed them anything else may fall in and become dinner themselves.

Head Giant Keeper
By Appointment to Her Majesty the Queen

'I is crodsquinkled!' yowled the Bloodbottler.

After the capture of the beastly giants, the BFG is given royal permission to blow his "phizzwizards" through the windows of sleeping children every night of the year.

The BFG
Royal Dream Blower

OFFICIAL RESIDENCE:
Giant's Green, Windsor Great Park
TEL: 976 1008   FAX: 976 1007

By Appointment to
HM The Queen

51

Fantastic Mr Fox

Beastly farmers Boggis, Bunce and Bean are tired of being outwitted by cunning Mr Fox. They plan to kill him, but they haven't realized quite how fantastic a fox he is – or to what lengths Mr Fox will go to protect his family.

The Fox Family

Mr Fox, his wife and four children live in a hole high up on a wooded hill. Every evening, the family feasts on chicken, duck, goose or turkey stolen by Mr Fox from the farms down below.

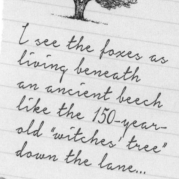

I see the foxes as living beneath an ancient beech like the 150-year-old "witches' tree" down the lane...

Boggis, Bunce and Bean

The three farmers that have it in for Mr Fox have quite revolting habits. Enormously fat Boggis eats three boiled chickens with dumplings a day, pot-bellied Bunce feasts on doughnuts stuffed with goose-liver paste, and pencil-thin Bean survives on nothing but strong cider.

'Boggis, Bunce and Bean
One fat, one short, one lean.'

My dear Boggis and Bunce

THAT LOUSY, THIEVING FOX MUST BE KILLED!

Meet me tomorrow in my orchard at noon, and I'll tell you how we can trap the brute in his hole — and get rid of him, once and for all!

Bean

BOGGIS'S BEST BIRDS

Premium Quality

FRESH PRODUCE

The Plumpest Chickens
Fed on the choicest grains, beetles and worms

Available at all Good Butchers

Perhaps the foxes could dig all the way to a supermarket? Or just get them digging to the 3 farms – and a permanent food supply?!

'Boggis's Chicken House Number One!'

cried Mr Fox. 'It's **exactly** what I was aiming at!'

Digging their way into the farmers' storehouses, the foxes discover a paradise for hungry animals!

'Stand and drink a toast to our dear friend who has saved our lives this day

– Mr Fox!'

Badger

My dear fellow hill-dwellers

Tonight you are all invited to a GRAND FEAST, courtesy of Messrs Boggis, Bunce and Bean.

– MENU –
Succulent chicken
Premium duck & goose
Smoked ham & bacon
And – for our rabbit friends – carrots!
The finest of cider will be available to wash it all down.

Mr and Mrs Fox

The Enormous Crocodile

Hungry for juicy children, the Enormous Crocodile is determined to catch at least three for lunch. He devises all sorts of cunning tricks, but the other animals are determined to put an end to this greedy brute's scheming, once and for all.

Humpy-Rumpy is the first animal to stop the Enormous Crocodile in his tracks.

'The sort of things that I'm going to eat
Have fingers, toe-nails, arms and legs and feet!'
THE ENORMOUS CROCODILE

DANGER!

Have You Seen This Croc?

There have been several reports of a crocodile behaving suspiciously in recent days. It has assumed various forms, including:

◎ **A coconut tree**

◎ **A see-saw**

◎ **A fairground ride**

PLEASE WATCH OUT FOR CUNNING CROCODILE BEHAVIOUR AND REMAIN VIGILANT AT ALL TIMES!

PRAISE FOR JUNGLE HEROES

▲ *Muggle-Wump described the croc as "horrid and hoggish".*

VILLAGE RESIDENTS HAVE BEEN SINGING the praises of several animals that – quite literally – snatched local children from the jaws of death.

The animals – a hippo, a monkey and a Roly-Poly bird – all gave warning of a crocodile poised to pounce.

School teacher Mrs Mahama described how her pupils were crowding round a "see-saw" when a monkey suddenly shouted, "Run, run, run!" As the screaming children scattered, she described how the "see-saw" waddled away into the bushes.

It is Trunky the elephant who has the last word when he sends the tricky croc into space!

The Giraffe and the Pelly and Me

Billy is fascinated by an empty sweet shop, the Grubber, that stands across the road from his home. One day he learns that a window-cleaning trio of a giraffe, a pelican and a monkey has moved in! When they ask for Billy's help, it is the start of a grand window-cleaning adventure.

The company's first request comes from His Grace The Duke of Hampshire.

Rewards for All

After the animals spot a burglar through a window, the grateful Duke invites all three to live on his estate for the rest of their lives – where there will be tinkle-tinkle blossoms for the Giraffe, walnuts for the Monkey and salmon for the Pelly. As for Billy, his greatest dream of all is about to come true...

Dear Sirs,

I saw your notice as I drove by this morning. I have been looking for a decent window-cleaner for the last 50 years but I have not found one yet. My house has 677 windows in it (not counting the greenhouses) and all of them are filthy. Kindly come and see me as soon as possible.

Yours truly,

Hampshire

POLICE REPORT

– THE CAPTURE OF COBRA –

Officers attended the Duke of Hampshire's estate where they found the Duke and Duchess with a small boy, a giraffe, a pelican and a monkey. After being informed that an armed villain had stolen the Duchess's jewels and was hiding in the pelican's beak, the burglar – commonly known as The Cobra – was apprehended inside said beak.

55

The Witches

Led by the terrifying Grand High Witch, *real* witches are everywhere – and they loathe children! Their mission is to sniff out youngsters and "make them disappear". However, one boy and his grandmother have a cunning plan get rid of these beastly beings, once and for all.

'A REAL WITCH gets the same pleasure from squelching a child as *you* get from eating a plateful of strawberries and thick cream.'

GRANDMAMMA

15 January

Ever since Mama and Papa had their accident, Grandmamma has been telling me stories about trolls and other magical stuff. Last night, she started talking about witches. She says they're all around us — and they look just like ordinary women!

Grandmamma says she has known five children here in Norway who were taken by witches. One, Birgit, turned into a chicken and laid huge eggs! Another, Harald, was turned into a little stone statue...

Grandmamma told me about how the Christiansen family woke one day to find their daughter missing from her bed. Later, her father spotted her trapped in this old painting that hung in the living room! She never came back.

PS:
I think Grandmamma's missing thumb might have something to do with the witches — but she won't say.

Grandmamma and me, Norway

I'm realizing that the boy's Grandmamma is just like my own wonderful grandmother!

English Witches

When Grandmamma and the boy leave Norway to live in England, she tells him that English witches are probably the "most vicious in the whole world". Their methods are extra-cunning, from turning children into slugs (so they can be squished by their own parents) to changing them into pheasants at the start of the shooting season.

Although they are hardly ever spotted, REAL WITCHES are everywhere.

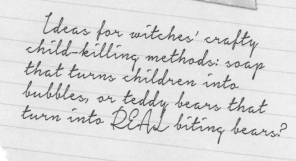

Ideas for witches' crafty child-killing methods: soap that turns children into bubbles, or teddy bears that turn into REAL biting bears?

The Hotel Magnificent

After the boy's grandmother is ill with pneumonia, the two – with the boy's pet mice, William and Mary – go on holiday to the English seaside town of Bournemouth. Here, at the Hotel Magnificent, the boy discovers just how vile and vicious English witches really are!

ⴵ HOTEL MAGNIFICENT ⴵ

RSPCC MEETING

STRICTLY PRIVATE!

This room is reserved for the Annual Meeting of

THE ROYAL SOCIETY FOR THE PREVENTION OF CRUELTY TO CHILDREN

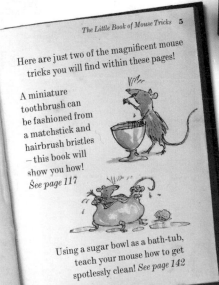

4   *The Little Book of Mouse Tricks*

→ Mouse Magic! ←

With a little time and devotion, you can train your mouse to perform any number of tricks. Teach your pet how to walk a tightrope, perform acrobatic feats or even brush his or her own teeth.

Amaze your family and friends! All you need is a mouse, The Little Book of Mouse Tricks – and plenty of patience!

The Little Book of Mouse Tricks   5

Here are just two of the magnificent mouse tricks you will find within these pages!

A miniature toothbrush can be fashioned from a matchstick and hairbrush bristles – this book will show you how! *See page 117*

Using a sugar bowl as a bath-tub, teach your mouse how to get spotlessly clean! *See page 142*

When the boy sneaks William and Mary into the hotel meeting room for a mouse-training session, matters are about to take a nasty turn…

'I demand maximum rrrree-sults! So here are my orders!
My orders are that every single child in this country shall be rrrubbed out,
squashed, squirted, squittered and frrrittered...
Do I make myself clear?'

THE GRAND HIGH WITCH

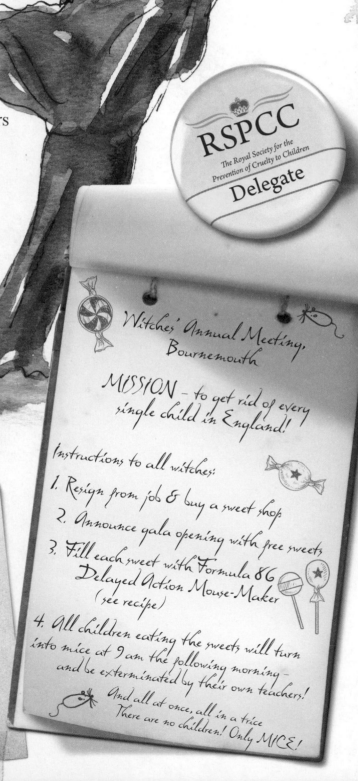

Stinky Children!

When the boy – hidden behind a screen – discovers that the RSPCC meeting is in fact a gathering of witches, he realizes he is in terrible danger. All children stink of dogs' droppings to witches, and can be sniffed out from a great distance...

ANNUAL MEETING
OF ENGLISH WITCHES

Miserable witches!
You are a heap of idle, good-for-nothing worms! I am seeing repulsive children everywhere. Why have you not rubbed them out? Have you forgotten the witches' mantra?!

Children are foul and filthy!

Children are dirty and stinky!

Children are smelling of dogs' droppings!

Down with children! Do them in!
Boil their bones and fry their skin!

You must take action. Listen carefully, write down everything I say - and **do not fail me**.

THE GRAND HIGH WITCH
OF ALL THE WORLD

58

RSPCC
The Royal Society for the
Prevention of Cruelty to Children
Delegate

Witches' Annual Meeting,
Bournemouth

MISSION – to get rid of every single child in England!

Instructions to all witches:

1. Resign from job & buy a sweet shop

2. Announce gala opening with free sweets

3. Fill each sweet with Formula 86 Delayed Action Mouse-Maker (see recipe)

4. All children eating the sweets will turn into mice at 9 am the following morning – and be exterminated by their own teachers!

And all at once, all in a trice
There are no children! Only MICE!

FORMULA 86
Delayed Action Mouse-Maker

INGREDIENTS

Wrong end of a telescope,
boiled for 21 hours

Alarm clock set for 9am,
roasted until crisp

45 brown mice

Frog juice

Gruntle's egg

Claw of a crabcruncher

Beak of a labbersnitch

Snout of a grobblesquirt

Tongue of a catspringer

METHOD

Chop off the mice-tails and fry
in hair-oil until crisp

Simmer the mice in frog juice

Using a high-speed mixer, blend
together the telescope, mice, tails and clock

Add in all the other ingredients, and
mix until you have a green liquid

Use 1 droplet per sweet

FORMULA 86 Delayed Action Mouse-Maker

Turned into Mice

The boy sees the Grand High Witch demonstrating the power of her marvellous recipe by changing Bruno Jenkins – a greedy boy staying at the hotel – into a mouse. And when the witches sniff out the boy, it's not long before he too is a mouse, scuttling around on the floor with Bruno.

As a mouse, the boy manages to steal a bottle of Mouse-Maker from the Grand High Witch's bedroom. Now to get it into the witches' dinner!

HOTEL MAGNIFICENT
- DINNER MENU -

Starter
Pea soup

RAPID RESPONSE
RODENT TERMINATION SERVICES
INVOICE 001003

Hotel Magnificent, Bournemouth

Call-out to severe
mouse infestation

Treatment and
extensive clear-up

BALANCE DUE: £300.00

Grandmamma made a call pretending to be the Norwegian chief of police and managed to get the Grand High Witch's address from the hotel register!

She lives in a castle here in Norway — so I can sneak in and find out the addresses of all the world's witches. I love being a mouse!

We will use mouse-maker — and cats — to get rid of the lot of them!

Grandmamma and me!

The End...